Free/DOM

Chrystina Lightfoot

 Presentation by *BookLeaf Publishing*

Web: www.bookleafpub.com

E-mail: info@bookleafpub.com

ISBN: 9789358368529

First edition 2024

To my momma. The OG.

ACKNOWLEDGEMENT

Chi-Miigwetch,
To MY people. The ones who always believe in me and take the time to listen to my crazy stories and continue to support me when I'm feeling lost.

PREFACE

You are truly remarkable...

Rewriting is the challenge

What is reality if you are the creator of your own narrative? Remember you are the narrator in your own story, within your own mind. Illustrate the ideas and thoughts that can become reality. Sit with that.

Find balance in your healing journey Ideas. Theories. Thoughts. Expand your intelligence. Reach to places you've never imagined.

Sharp

You are like steel, a sword is made from
It may take some bearings but it has a
shine to it at the end of the day.

You can take fire to the sword and reshape,
reform, and sharpen–oh but how it will
never feel or look the same.
Alternating it may not cause any more
clarity.

Environment

Set the tone. The vibe. The feelings.
Reflect on the work.
Take care of your surroundings.
Allowing nature to take its personal course
one day at a time.
Clouds, Stars, and living organisms
surround us with reminders and signs that
we are walking along the journey to
enlightenment. Seek your environment.

Be kind to yourself

Focus on your power, the gift,
the one you keep running from

It's uncomfortable. We know.
When you are aligned with your values,
morals, and ethics...it can feel eerie
because the unknown is so uncomfortable
but when it starts to become familiar
embrace it.

Let it become the new normal.

Mind

I love my mind.
I love my body.
I love my layers, which create the warmth
of the evening nights.
Humor me.
Make me laugh.
Challenge my brain and bring me peace-
let my mind wander too.

Searching for peace, no more harassment
and injustice, no more hovering over your
shoulder, while everyone else gets to sleep.
We weep, we hold sorrow
That continues to creep within the weak

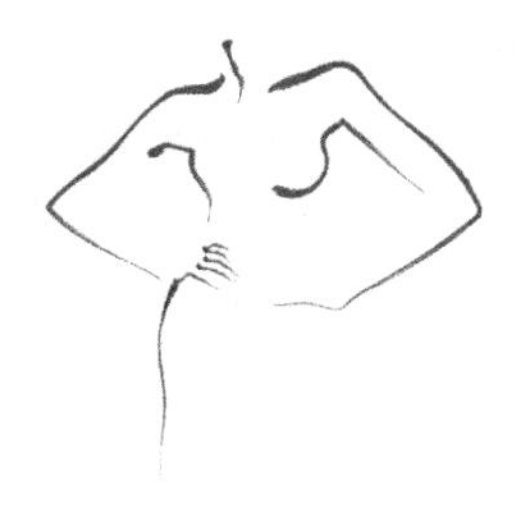

Obstacles

Walls, chambers, and gates
that hold us from seeing our growth. Do we
block our own natural flow to success?
I wonder at times if my mind or the outside
world is the real peace, hard to tell at times

Create plan C, when A and B don't feel
right
These obstacles are larger in your mind
even when you feel so small..

Imprisonment is where my mind can feel
at times. Either way peace is a choice
within. Ask what your anger is showing
you, what do you need right now?

Grateful

Blessed is what some call it
Good Karma for others
Some call it luck within the social
construct
Spirituality is my current location within
However, All I know is that I am...

Repeating History

What people struggle with is asking,
Not telling someone that they need
assistance

Feeling vulnerable does not make you
weak.
We can't allow our blood to bleed through
and leak all over and not expect it to seep,
internally to those around us.

We humans can restructure society and
learn how to find compassion again, let's
break the cycle and not repeat it anymore.

I'm tired. Survival to revival; some days it's
hard to tell where I am.

-Let's heal and take pride in our scars, let's
not feel so incomplete anymore.

Inner Voice

Who created those negative words and statements?
Inhale confidence
Exhale doubt
Don't ever let your thoughts consume your peace.

Ego can lead for years
Barriers, create fears
Spirits protect you, don't be afraid
May I ask why it hurts so bad in that inner voice of yours?

That or This
This or That

Consequences or Experiences
Wisdom or Life Lessons
Changes or Stagnant
Alone or Lonely
Opportunity or Fear
Dark or Light
Unstable or unable?
Welfare or Warfare
Meditate or Medicate?

You are the
Heart on my sleeve

You teach patience.
You show kindness.
You pour love.
You have no problem showing your raw emotions.
Strong built for a perfectly chaotic minded woman,
Creating space to be comfortable
No matter what, no matter where... I will always care and love the individual you are and hold that space here.

Impact

Feeling is the only intuition you can follow.
What makes you feel good?
Minimize your space to maximize your mind.

"When it rains it pours" is the saying, however, you can always share an umbrella when it storms.

Create space when you feel lonely
More people are attracted to the light than the dark. Don't lose that sense of wonder in life, keep cultivating awe at the wonder of existence. Relearn, decolonize yourself. Let that authenticity lead and let go.

Dimensional

When freedom is being threatened how can we flip the script and rewrite history in a positive way?

Are you quiet because you are calm? Or are you scared?
Or is it because I made you uncomfortable?
Move more like water, free.
Not like fire, where it can engulf in seconds and take over.

Roots

Multicultural; multi-meaning more than
one or two.
This is who I am; blending the cultures
together to find a beautiful mosaic
completed piece.

The roots are held beneath the earth
Rooted in culture that bleeds within my
veins
Strong
Hold the world together strand by strand;
Planted- For lifetimes to come

Bravery

The wind is strong and warm from the south.
Reminding you of the summer months, when the sun shines harder. You absorb the rays, building up the energy from within.

Determined to grow, from interpersonal relationships. I am calming down. The anger isn't holding me back anymore. I can be brave now.

Lakes

Water is life
Humans are water
Animals need an ecosystem to survive,
where they can create a space to thrive.
Drifting, east
The breeze from the lakes move
throughout the land. Breathe in the cold
air. A fresh new start,
At last, we are at the *Great Lakes.*

South Wind

The name that has taken its own journey in self-discovery.
When I struggle the most, the wind reminds me of my ancestors; Who felt the same warm wind come across their bodies, throughout all the struggles that they overcame.

I am here because of them and continue to be for my descendants after.

Mask Off

~Tiger Mask
Removed from the grasslands and tropical forest
Tempestuous and fearsome at times,
she comes across as courageous but with the mask on or off the tiger can be seen as scary and still can show up at unexpected times and places.
Withdrawn from society, it can be a lonely journey walking strong for so long. I am ready to take the tiger mask off. However, the stripes will always be there to remind me of my journey.

Silence or Fear

Colorism within your own race, ethnicity,
and tribe.
Elders are our wisdom
We are extensions of our roots and
environments.
Killer, of the silence
We are the voices for those who can't.
We are the voices of our children to come,
that's when I speak.
Listen, actively over reasonable efforts is
how we move in the system
Who are we?
The system isn't created for people of color

It's created to hold us back, we are human,
how have we let it become like this?
Why are we letting it continue for
generations to come
How do we heal from this trauma?

Align within yourself.

Align within yourself.

Align within yourself.

Align within yourself.

Align within yourself.

Privilege

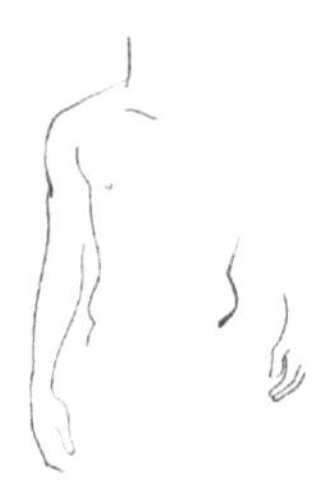

White
Male
Heterosexual
Wealthy

These are the conditions that the westernized culture has created for decades to be of the pristine labels.

We have no control over the family we are born into or the color of our skin. We hold many tones and shades.
I am a half-breed; a hafu with light skin
Tell me where I fall in line, because I am the next of kin.

My body is a shell that my energy fills and
once my body is at rest, my strength
continues, I am still

Searching

For peace,

For my people, for all people, we are the people

Searching for tranquility and all the stability while my make believe inabilities take a hold on me

Life has taught me humility while others choose arrogance and it's evident.

All wanting the inheritance and not realizing it's ending the teachings, how did we get so

attached to the monetary value of things,
that we can not take with us.

I see a beautiful figure in the distance, just a
dark silhouette and it just reminds me of our
very existence in this chaotic world. Oh,
how if we could all just see silhouettes
instead and not the shades of melanin.

Selective

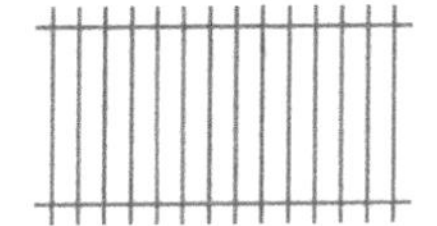

On who I am around, cause please find me
a reason to keep you near because I ain't
seeing it very clear, with all this baggage
you make me carry, it's not mine to hold

I have to be protective over my body, mind,
and energy. You can't keep taking and not
refill the glass and then act mistaken for
how I treat you with silence.

I am selective; but how is it frowned upon
when us civilians do it?

We live in a society where our police can take lives and be selective on the shades with no repercussions.
However, when we speak it's left with no discussions and only interruptions.
Complaints, it's just a cop out while the cops can stay out. Back off, I'm staying selective with no doubt.

Human

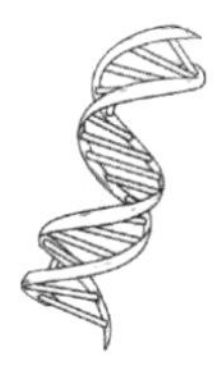

Interconnectedness
Intertwined with one another and nature.
I am human. One of a kind. Uniquely made in my DNA.

The pressure we put upon ourselves can be hard to overcome, but remember, pressure can make diamonds but it also can make coal. It's all a mindset at the end of the day.

Stressing to the point of pressin'
Reaching for revival from all this survival

I am human and tired of repressing
my thoughts and ideas because they
don't fit in the conformity of what the
majority wants because I am the
minority. I am human.

Reset

I am hurt; I am angry; I am furious
But just like the seasons, winter does come
to an end. While she is resting; I am
resetting.

When spring starts to show; birds are
chirping and the sun rays are seeping into
our veins and into our heart. I hear our
Mother Earth wake up again.

Madness is only prolonged sadness that
can turn into brilliance and grace with a flip
of a perspective.

Just like the moon it can shine without the
sun. My anger shall pass and my love for
myself will come back to one.

Hurtful

I'm screaming in the woods to find peace and tranquility; however, I just find myself in a cell staring at corruptibility.

My body was thrown into solitary confinement, white walls to stare at. Shivering in my own anger, realizing I am no different.

I want to scream so loud till I can't breathe, with every ounce of hurt leaving my body. The next breath I take will only be fresh new beginnings. I am no longer hurting. I am fully living; I am a human being.

Capable

You are.

Printed in the USA
CPSIA information can be obtained
at www.ICGtesting.com
CBHW061155120624
9957CB00010B/627